CORAL

by

Corey Anne Abreau

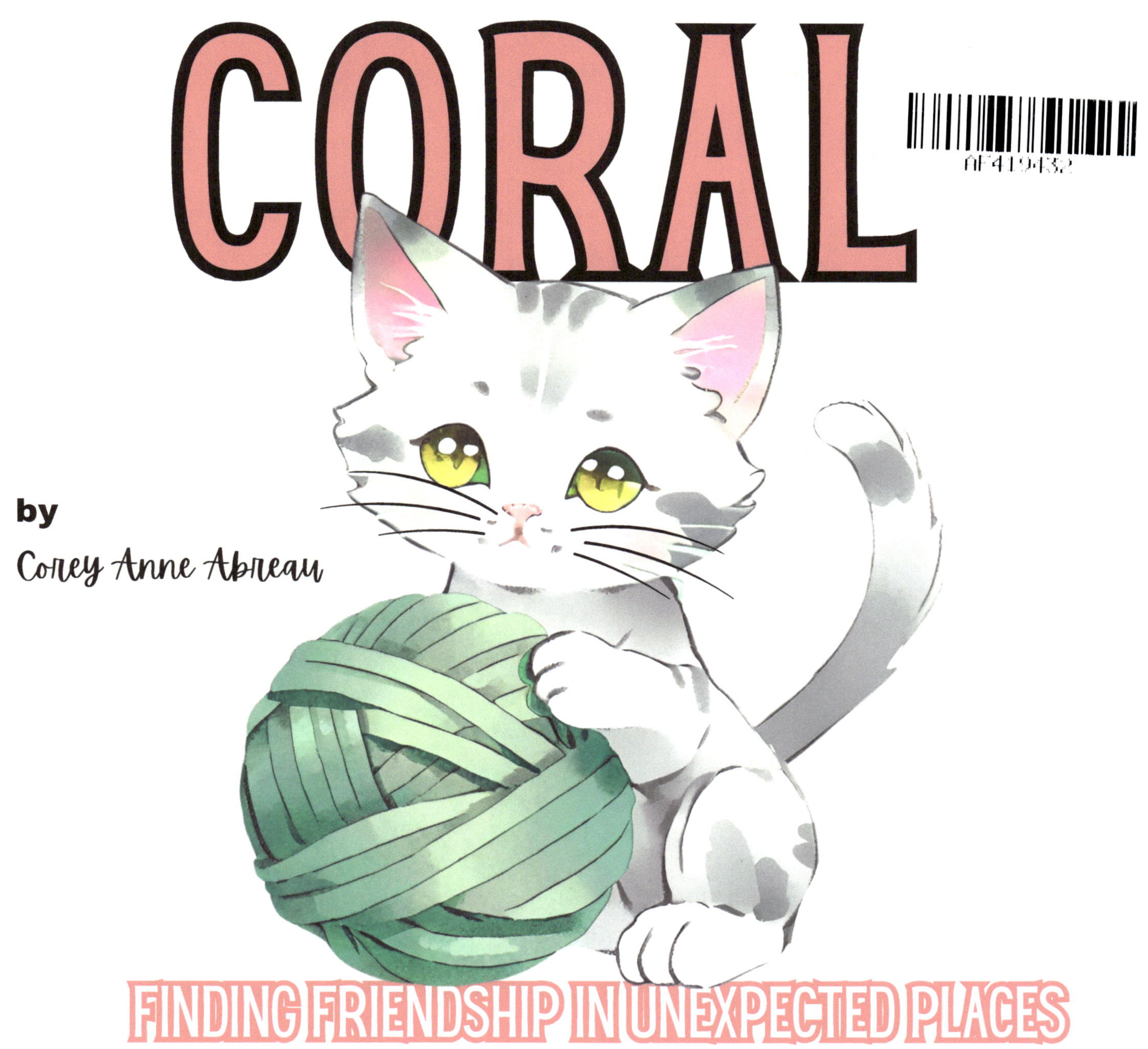

FINDING FRIENDSHIP IN UNEXPECTED PLACES

For
Cole, Carter, & Coral

Copyright © 2024 Corey Anne Abreau

All rights reserved. No part of this publication may be reproduced, distributed, or transmitted in any form or by any means, including photocopying, recording, or other electronic mechanical methods, without the prior written permission of the author and/or publisher, except in the case of brief quotations in a book review. For permission, you may email coreyabreau@gmail.com.

CORAL

FINDING FRIENDSHIP IN UNEXPECTED PLACES

In a cozy house on the edge of town, there lived two brothers named Cole and Carter.

They were the best of friends, sharing everything from toys to dreams, and their days were filled with sunshine and laughter.

In spite of the age difference between the brothers, they formed a close relationship.

Then, one day, something happened that changed everything. Cole, the older brother, received an exciting opportunity to go to a faraway place for school.

While Carter was happy for Cole, his heart felt heavy at the thought of being apart from his brother.

Cole's departure day approached quickly, the house grew quieter, and Carter's smile became a little less bright.

Seeing her youngest son's sadness, Mom knew she had to do something to help him through this time. So, she came up with a plan. A new and exciting change was about to happen in their home, something Carter did not expect.

That afternoon, Mom walked in with a mysterious box in her hands. "Carter," Mom said with a twinkle in her eye, "I have a surprise for you!"

Carter's eyes widened with curiosity as Mom carefully opened the box, revealing a fluffy fur bundle inside. "Meow!" came a tiny voice, and an adorable kitten with soft gray fur and bright green eyes popped out.

"Wow! Can I hold her, Mom? Can I?" Carter exclaimed, his excitement bubbling over.

"You sure can!" Mom nodded with a smile, and Carter gently scooped up the kitten, feeling her tiny heartbeat against his chest. "Thank you so much, Mom. But wait, what should we name her?" he wondered aloud.

CAT FOOD

Mom chuckled and suggested, "How about Buttons? She has the cutest button nose. Or perhaps Coral?"

"I think she looks like a gray squirrel cat," Carter laughed. "Coral The Gray Squirrel Cat it will be."

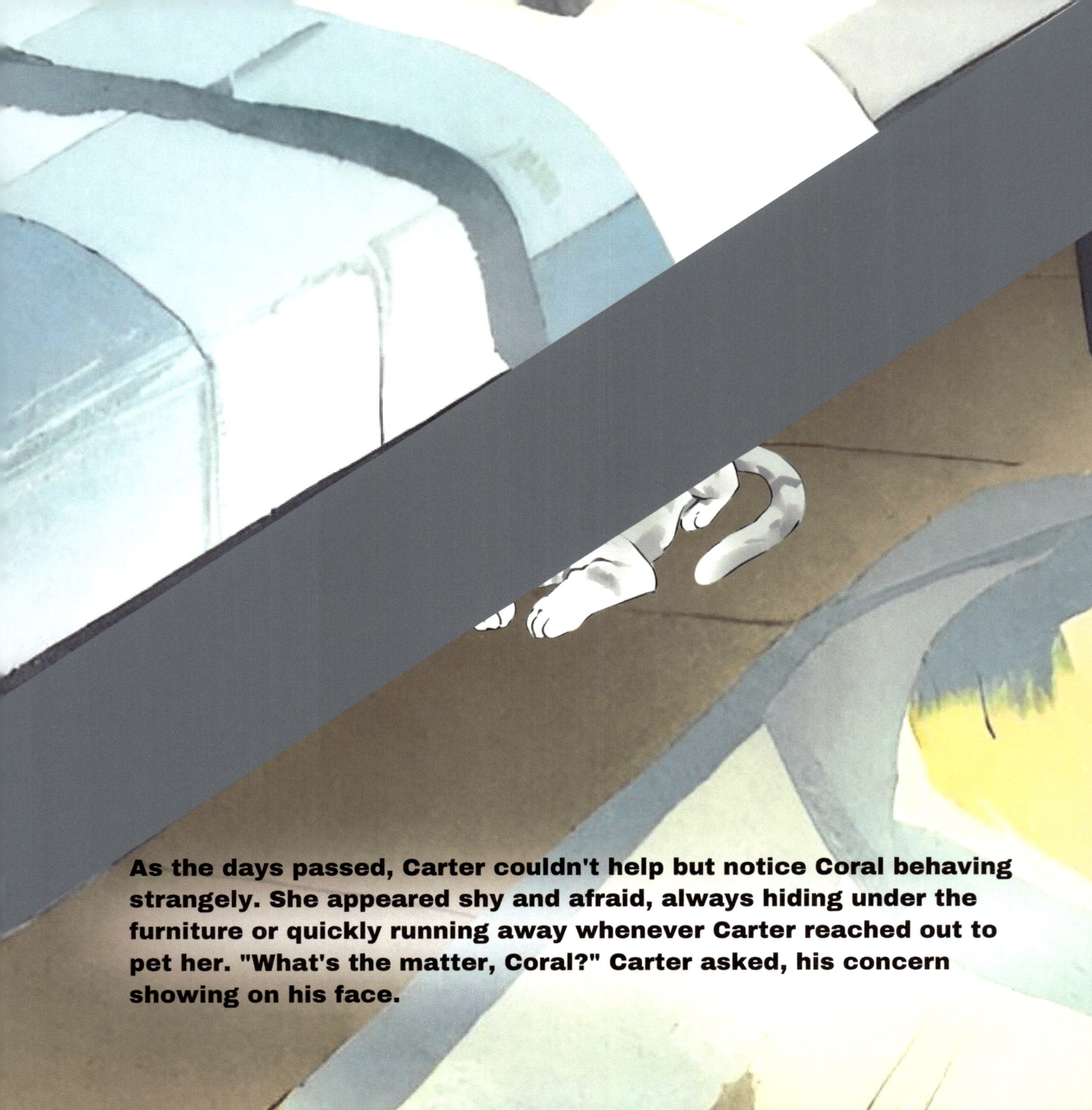

As the days passed, Carter couldn't help but notice Coral behaving strangely. She appeared shy and afraid, always hiding under the furniture or quickly running away whenever Carter reached out to pet her. "What's the matter, Coral?" Carter asked, his concern showing on his face.

Mom knelt down beside him, her gaze gentle. "It seems Coral might be a bit scared, honey," she explained softly. "Perhaps she needs some time to adjust to her new home and to us." Carter nodded thoughtfully, determined to help Coral feel safe and loved.

He spent hours sitting quietly near her hiding spot, but she wouldn't come out.

He tried speaking softly to her to help her feel more at ease, but she wouldn't move.

She went deeper into her hiding spot.

Seeing Coral hiding made Carter feel worried and a little sad.

That night before bed, Carter decided to give his brother a call and see if they could put their heads together about how to help Coral.

Cole said, "Be patient with her. It will take a little time for her to warm up to you, but don't give up, little bro. You've got this."

That next morning, Carter woke up with an idea. He thought and thought all night about what else he could try, he exclaimed, "I've got it! I'll offer treats and toys to encourage Coral out of her hiding spot."

Slowly but surely, it worked. Coral would creep her head out of her hiding spot to sniff his hand or bat her paw playfully at a string he dangled for her.

Carter remained still for a moment, offering Coral the space and time she needed to make her approach.

As the days went by, Coral and Carter grew closer,
and she gradually learned to trust him.

They played hide and seek, raced around the house, and even took naps together on the couch.

That evening, Carter called Cole again. "You'll never guess who's on my lap right now!" he exclaimed.

Cole pondered for a moment before responding, "Hmm, could it possibly be Coral?" They both chuckled, and Cole continued, "That's fantastic, Carter. I'm incredibly proud of you for persevering and not giving up."

As the brothers hung up the phone, Carter felt a mix of emotions swirling inside him. But, amidst the uncertainty, a glimmer of hope shined through. Gazing into Coral's eyes, he experienced a moment of profound realization: while one door may close, another always opens.

With Coral The Gray Squirrel Cat by his side, Carter knew that even though his big brother was far away, a new chapter of adventure and friendship awaited him and Coral.

As they snuggled together that night, Carter whispered words of gratitude to Coral. "Thank you for being my friend," he said, his voice filled with love. "No matter what lies ahead, we'll face each challenge hand in paw."

How many of these Cute Books 4 kids have you read?

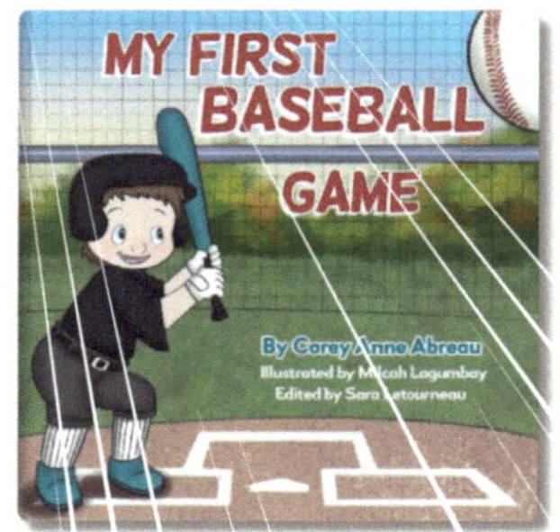

Cat Chore Chart

	Mon	Tues	Wed	Thurs	Fri	Sat	Sun
FOOD							
FRESH WATER							
SCOOP LITER BOX							
PLAY							
GROOM							

Corey Anne Abreau
cutebooks4kids.net

www.ingramcontent.com/pod-product-compliance
Lightning Source LLC
Chambersburg PA
CBHW041627110726

48005CB00002B/523